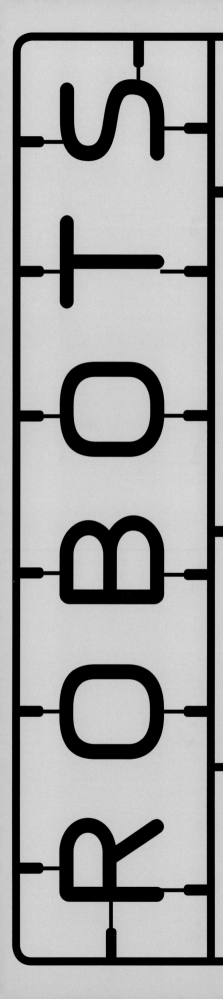

ROBOTS

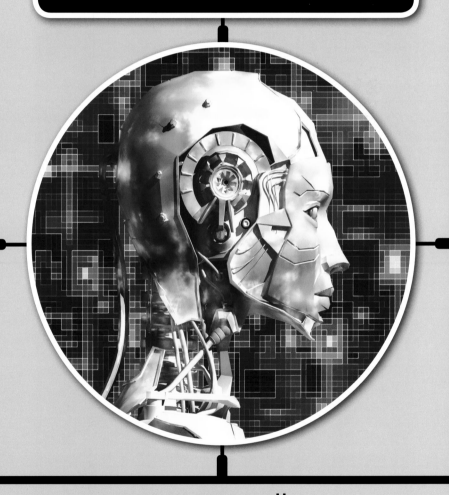

ADVENTURES IN STEAM

Izzi Howell

Fact Finders®

CAPSTONE PRESS
a capstone imprint

Fact Finders Books are published by Capstone Press,
1710 Roe Crest Drive, North Mankato, Minnesota 56003
www.mycapstone.com

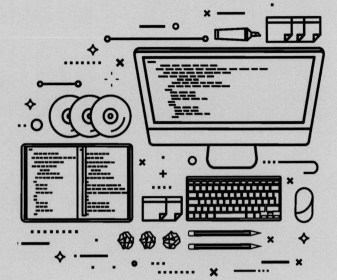

Library of Congress Cataloging-in-Publication Data
Library of Congress Cataloging-in-Publication data is
available on the Library of Congress website.
ISBN: 978-1-5435-3231-9 (library binding)
ISBN: 978-1-5435-3547-1 (paperback)
ISBN: 978-1-5435-3553-2 (eBook PDF)

Summary: Closely ties into the STEAM initiative by
offering an overview of the many types of robots in use
today and explaining how they work. From drones and
space rovers to bionic arms and androids, robots are becoming more prevalent in our world.

Editorial Credits
Series editor: Izzi Howell
Designer: Rocket Design (East Anglia) Ltd
Illustrations: Rocket Design (East Anglia) Ltd
In-house editor: Julia Bird/Catherine Brereton

Photo Credits
Alamy: Xinhua 31c, REUTERS 32br and 33b, Paolo Patrizi 40; Dreamstime: Theowl84 11; iStock:
VLADGRIN 19, JasonDoiy 29, CatLane 32bl, brittak 36t, Woodkern 45; Jean-Michel Mongeau, Ardian
Jusufi and Pauline Jennings. Courtesy of PolyPEDAL Lab UC Berkeley 6; Julian Baker 37; NASA: 27,
NASA/JPL-Caltech/MSSS 30t; Shutterstock: NesaCera cover and title page, OlegDoroshin 4, Designua
12, Alena Kirdina 13, Scanrail1 16, Christian Mueller 17, LANTERIA 18, Nataliya Hora 20, Tatiana
Shepeleva 21, Tim Jenner 22, Everett Historical 23b, Lerner Vadim 25, Miks Mihails Ignats, Alex
Tuzhikov, B Brown, anucha sirivisansuwan 28 l-r, catwalker 30b, chuckstock 31t, Quality Stock Arts 32t,
CHEN WS 33tl, iLoveCoffeeDesign 34, Tyler Olson 35, Aleks Melnik 36b, s_bukley 42t, Featureflash
Photo Agency 42br, Sarunyu L 42bc, Nicescene 42bl, Anton_Ivanov 43t, Phillip Maguire 43c,
Wasan Ritthawon 43b, Ramona Kaulitzki 44; Wikimedia: Daderot 23t, Copyright Georgia Institute of
Technology 2008/Rob Felt 24, Tactical Technology Office, Defense Advanced Research Projects Agency,
U.S. Department of Defense 31b, Sven Volkens 32c.

All design elements from Shutterstock.

First published in Great Britain in 2017 by Wayland

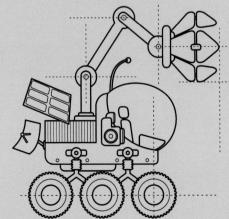

Printed and bound in China at WKT Company Ltd.

TABLE OF CONTENTS

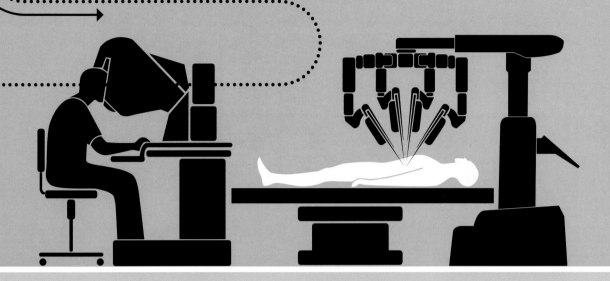

DESIGNING A ROBOT

A ROBOT IS A MACHINE THAT CAN BE **PROGRAMMED** TO ACT IN A CERTAIN WAY. ROBOTS USE **SENSORS** TO GATHER INFORMATION ABOUT THEIR ENVIRONMENT. THEY ARE PROGRAMMED TO USE THIS INFORMATION TO DECIDE HOW TO ACT.

Robots have many functions. They can help humans with tasks as varied as working in factories, performing surgery, and exploring the Antarctic. Whatever the final purpose of the robot, the planning process is the same.

STEP 1

CONCEPT
What is the purpose of the robot? What features does it need? What size does it need to be?

STEP 2

DESIGN
How will the robot fulfill the aims set out in the concept? What will it look like? How can we make the robot move in the right way? How can we program it to behave correctly?

STEP 3

CREATION
How can the design be converted into a real robot? What parts do we need? How long will it take to put together?

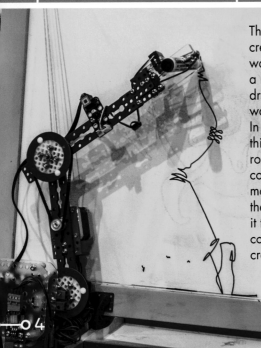

The designers who created this robot wanted to make a robot that could draw a picture. This was their concept. In order to achieve this, they gave the robot parts that could hold and move a pen. Then, they programmed it to move in the correct way to create a drawing.

PROJECT

- Look at the photo of the robot that can draw. How could you adapt this robot so it could paint a wall?

- Which parts of the robot need to change?

- Which parts can stay the same?

- How could you adapt it further so that it could paint *and* draw?

T TAKES MANY DIFFERENT SKILLS TO DESIGN AND CREATE ROBOTS. SOME ROBOTS ARE MADE BY LARGE TEAMS OF PEOPLE, WHILE OTHERS ARE PUT TOGETHER BY ONE PERSON WORKING VERY HARD ON THEIR OWN.

1

Experts provide a brief for what they need the robot to be able to do.

2

Mechanical engineers design the body of the robot. They think about how it needs to move and how it can sense its environment.

3
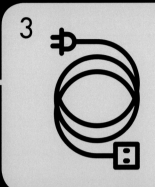

Electrical engineers design the **electrical circuits** that power the robot.

4
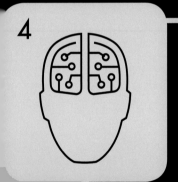

Software engineers program the computer of the robot. Programming a robot means that it can react in the right way to information from its sensors.

TECHNOLOGY TALK

Computer programs make life easier for electrical and mechanical engineers by allowing them to plan and test the structure and electrical circuits of a robot before it is built. 3D printers can also be used to print individual robot parts, whether they are large and difficult to construct or small and detailed.

5

Mechanics put together the pieces that make up the robot and test that it works properly.

MOVING PARTS

A ROBOT HAS MECHANICAL PARTS THAT FIT TOGETHER AND ALLOW IT TO MOVE, JUST LIKE THE SKELETON AND MUSCLES OF AN ANIMAL. THE WAY IN WHICH A ROBOT MOVES DEPENDS ON ITS FUNCTION AND WHERE IT WILL BE USED.

Every day we move in thousands of ways without giving much thought to how our bodies allow us to do so. Even a simple movement, such as picking up a pen, requires us to bend and stretch many connected bones and muscles. During the design process, mechanical engineers have to consider how a robot will **interact** with its environment. A robot will only be able to carry out complex movements if it has a mechanical structure that allows it to do so.

Engineers also have to plan how robots will get around. It is very complicated to create a robot that can walk on two feet. Rolling on wheels is much easier and quicker, but there is one big drawback—wheeled robots can't go up stairs.

The tiny, six-legged DASH robot can flip under a ledge and run along its underside, just like a cockroach. Its designers wanted to create a robot that could explore the rubble of collapsed buildings. They were inspired by the way cockroaches can scramble over uneven ground.

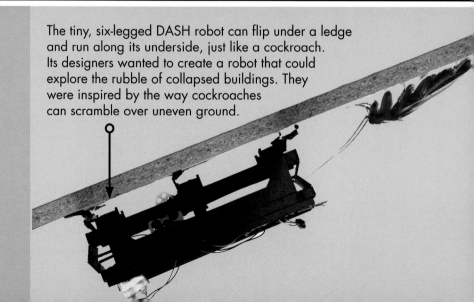

THINKING OUTSIDE THE BOX!

Scientists have designed other robots that mimic the way animals move. For example, the underwater exploration robot Crabster CR200 crawls along the ocean floor like a crab. It can adjust the position of each of its six legs individually to keep its balance in strong ocean currents.

MATH TALK

Engineers use triangles to figure out the angle at which robot arms need to bend. If you mark a point at the top of a robot arm, the middle of the arm joint, and at the point the robot needs to reach, it forms a triangle.

45 degrees   **80 degrees**

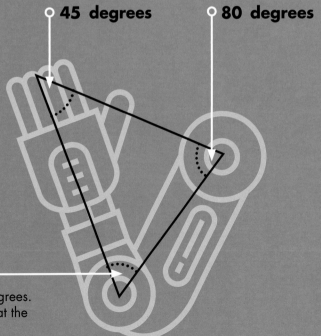

All the angles in a triangle add up to 180 degrees. Use this information to figure out the angle that the elbow joint of this robot arm needs to bend.

CIRCUITS

IF MECHANICAL PARTS ARE THE SKELETON AND MUSCLES OF A ROBOT, ELECTRICITY IS ITS BLOOD. ELECTRICITY GIVES ROBOTS THE POWER TO MOVE AND CARRY OUT ACTIONS.

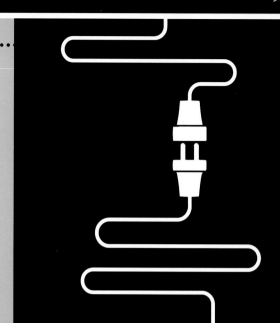

Most robots are fitted with internal electrical cables that carry electricity around the machine and power its components. These cables are arranged in circuits. If a circuit is not complete, electricity will not flow around the robot, and it will stop working.

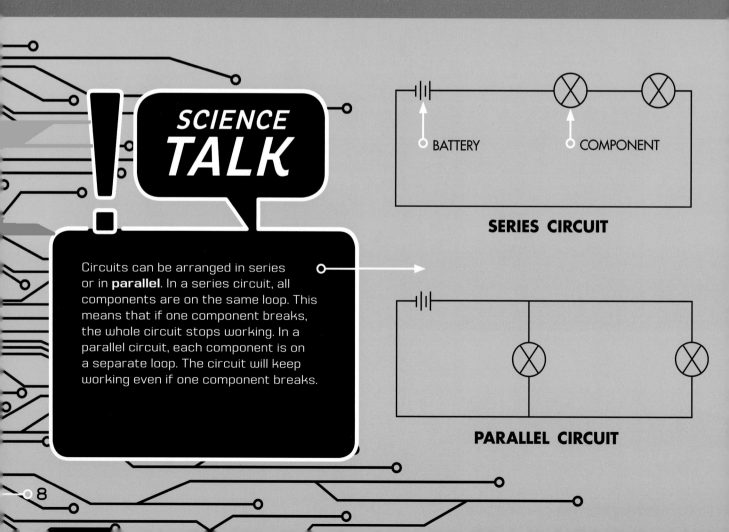

SCIENCE TALK

Circuits can be arranged in series or in **parallel**. In a series circuit, all components are on the same loop. This means that if one component breaks, the whole circuit stops working. In a parallel circuit, each component is on a separate loop. The circuit will keep working even if one component breaks.

BATTERY COMPONENT

SERIES CIRCUIT

PARALLEL CIRCUIT

Robots need to be connected to a power source that will send electricity around their circuits. Plugging a robot into an electrical outlet is an easy way to access a lot of electricity. But it limits the movement of the robot because it can't move too far away from the socket. Battery-powered robots can travel freely, but their batteries will eventually need to be recharged or replaced.

Small robots can be powered by household batteries.

THINKING OUTSIDE THE BOX!

Robots in space can't connect to electrical outlets or have their batteries replaced, so they often run on solar power instead. The solar panels on the robot convert light from the sun into a constant supply of electricity—as long as the robot isn't covered or in darkness. Some robots can also get energy from food. Scientists have created **prototypes** for a grass-eating lawnmower robot and a slug-eating robot, which would be very popular with gardeners!

SENSORS

MOST ROBOTS HAVE ELECTRICAL SENSORS THAT THEY USE TO GATHER INFORMATION ABOUT THE WORLD AROUND THEM, JUST AS HUMANS DO THROUGH OUR SENSES. SOME ROBOTS CAN EVEN SENSE THINGS THAT HUMANS CANNOT, SUCH AS X-RAYS AND MAGNETISM.

A sensor is a device that gathers information. Not all sensors are electrical, though. For example, an ear is a **biological** sensor that humans and animals use to sense sounds, or hear. Instead of ears, robots use microphones to sense sounds around them.

TECHNOLOGY TALK

To sense sounds, robots record noise with their microphones and convert the noise into signals that show the pitch and strength of the sound. The robot's computer then looks through a **database** of sound patterns to recognize the words or type of noise. This process is the same as that used by the voice recognition software on your home computer or smartphone.

This diagram shows the sound waves produced by a person speaking. This is the type of pattern that computers analyze to identify what someone is saying. This pattern shows someone saying "I love you." Can you make out where each word appears in the pattern?

Proprioception, or the sense of your own movement and position, is a little-known yet highly important sense for humans and robots alike. Robots can estimate how they are moving by measuring their own speed and rotation and using pressure sensors to monitor things that they touch.

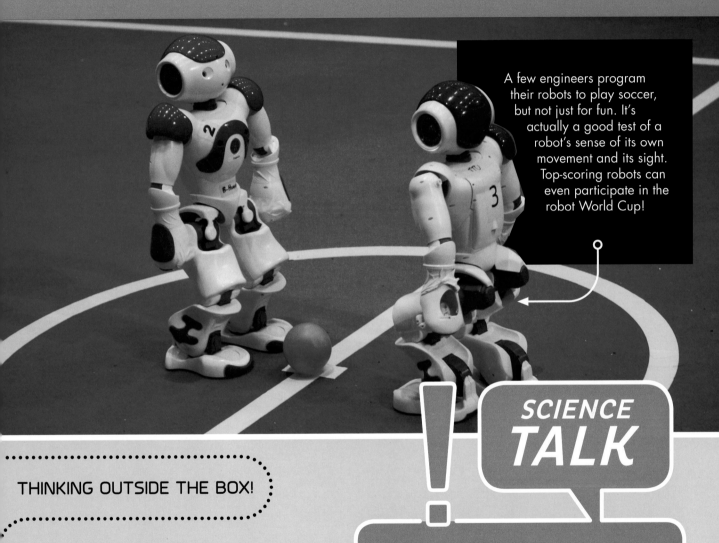

A few engineers program their robots to play soccer, but not just for fun. It's actually a good test of a robot's sense of its own movement and its sight. Top-scoring robots can even participate in the robot World Cup!

THINKING OUTSIDE THE BOX!

Any sensor that can be built can be added to a robot. This gives robots an almost unlimited number of possible senses. Robots can be given special sensors to sense temperature or find magnetic materials and rocks. They can even identify things that are invisible to humans, such as radio waves and X-rays.

SCIENCE TALK

Our sense of smell is actually just chemistry because sensors in the nose recognize the tiny chemical **molecules** given off by objects. Robots with similar electrical sensors can recognize smells in the same way. Mexican scientist Blanca Lorena Villareal has gone a step further. She is developing a robot that can follow certain smells, such as blood and sweat during search-and-rescue missions.

SIGHT AND NAVIGATION

SOME ROBOTS NEED TO BE ABLE TO **NAVIGATE** THEIR PHYSICAL ENVIRONMENT, SO THAT HUMANS DON'T HAVE TO MANUALLY DIRECT THEM. GIVING ROBOTS THE SENSE OF SIGHT ISN'T THE ONLY WAY TO DO THIS. SOUND CAN ALSO BE A USEFUL NAVIGATIONAL TOOL.

One way to give robots a sense of what is around them is to use **sonar**. With sonar a sender makes a noise and sends out a sound wave. The sound wave bounces off nearby objects and is reflected back to the sender. The sender's sensor (such as an ear) interprets the reflected sound wave and builds up a picture of its physical environment. Self-driving cars, which mainly use **GPS** to navigate the roads, also have sonar to warn them of unexpected obstacles.

THINKING OUTSIDE THE BOX!

Scientists are often inspired by nature. The idea for sonar came from animals that naturally use sonar, or echolocation, to navigate and find food. Bats have very poor vision, so they use echolocation to search for insects to eat while they are hunting at night. Echolocation also helps dolphins and porpoises find fish underwater where their vision is limited.

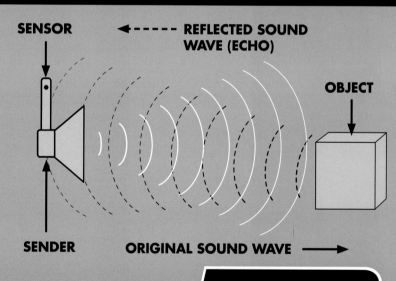

SENSOR ◄----- REFLECTED SOUND WAVE (ECHO)

OBJECT

SENDER   ORIGINAL SOUND WAVE →

PROJECT

■ Try using echolocation to navigate around a room. Blindfold yourself and communicate with a partner, who is hiding, by using sound. When you say a word, your partner must echo it back. See how long it takes for you to find your partner.

■ How can you tell when your partner is far away?

■ What does it sound like when your partner is close?

■ Which objects in the room confuse your sense of where your partner is?

Sonar and GPS let robots know that there are objects around them, but they can't help robots identify what those objects are. Some robots can be programmed to use visual information from a camera to recognize objects. Human brains can automatically identify familiar objects on sight. But robots need to be taught what shapes to look out for, as well as the names that we give those objects.

ENGINEERING TALK

If a person sees a table from any angle, they automatically recognize it as a table. However, a robot will need to be taught to recognize the combination of shapes as a table. Engineers do this by programming robots with databases of information that describes many possible shapes and their meanings.

If a robot sees a 4.8-inch (12-centimeter) tall cylinder, it can consult its database to figure out that the object is a soda can. However, if the can is crushed or at a different angle, complex programs called neutral networks are pretty good at recognizing it. But they can't tell how the can got that way or why.

CODE

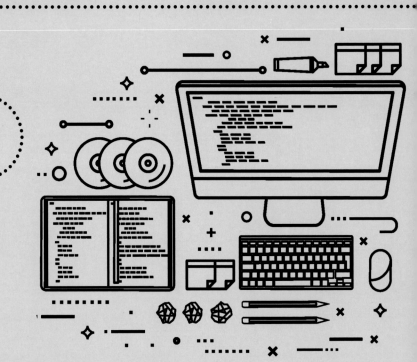

COMPLEX COMPUTER PROGRAMMING IS WHAT SETS ROBOTS APART FROM SIMPLE MACHINES, SUCH AS HAIR DRYERS. COMPUTERS ARE THE "BRAINS" OF ROBOTS, TELLING THEM WHAT TO DO AND HOW TO DO IT.

Software engineers write instructions for computers using **code**, which is a special type of language. Anything that is connected to a computer—from computer games to phone apps to robots—runs on code.

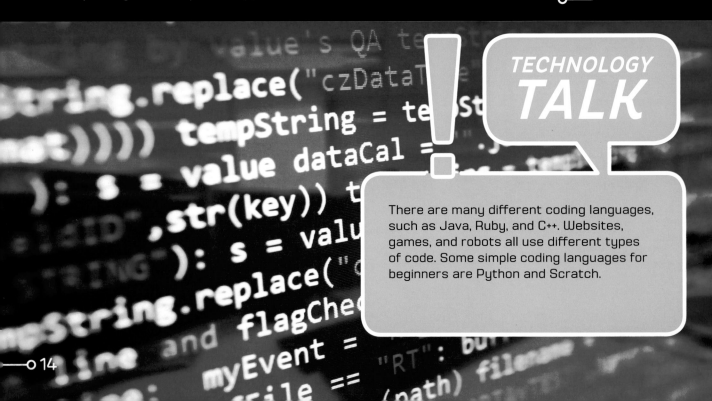

TECHNOLOGY TALK

There are many different coding languages, such as Java, Ruby, and C++. Websites, games, and robots all use different types of code. Some simple coding languages for beginners are Python and Scratch.

When a coder writes instructions for a task for a robot, the instructions have to be broken down into small steps. For example, rather than saying "make toast," you would need to explain step-by-step exactly how to make toast. Computers won't do anything unless you instruct them to, so it's important to include everything that you want them to do.

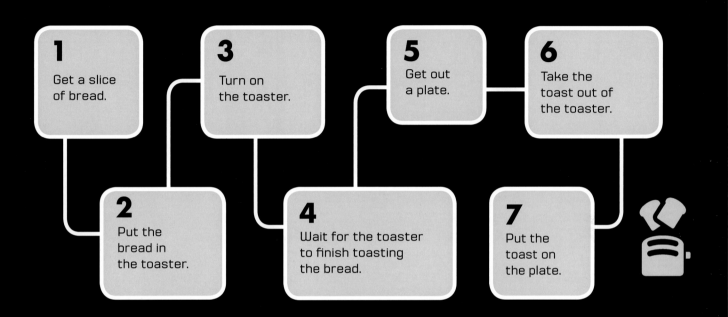

1 Get a slice of bread.

2 Put the bread in the toaster.

3 Turn on the toaster.

4 Wait for the toaster to finish toasting the bread.

5 Get out a plate.

6 Take the toast out of the toaster.

7 Put the toast on the plate.

MATH TALK

Computers need to be told in what order they should carry out their instructions, or the task will go wrong. This is the same when you work out long equations in math with multiple operations. For example, the answer to 5 + 2 x 4 could be 28 or 13, depending on whether you add or multiply first. The rules of operation state that you should do multiplication or division first and then addition or subtraction. What is the correct answer to 5 + 2 x 4?

ERROR!

PROJECT

- Write a code for an activity that you do every day, such as brushing your teeth or making your bed. Make sure that you break down every step.

- How many steps does it take?

- How easy would it be for a robot to follow your instructions?

PROGRAMMING ROBOTS

THE COMPUTER INSIDE A ROBOT IS PROGRAMMED TO MAKE DECISIONS USING INFORMATION GATHERED FROM ITS SENSORS. BUT ROBOTS CAN ONLY DO THINGS THAT THEY HAVE BEEN PROGRAMMED TO DO. THEY CANNOT CHOOSE TO DO THINGS ON THEIR OWN.

The way in which robots are programmed to make decisions is just like a flowchart. The stages of the flowchart show different decisions that a robot could make. For example, this flowchart shows how a robot could be programmed to cross the street.

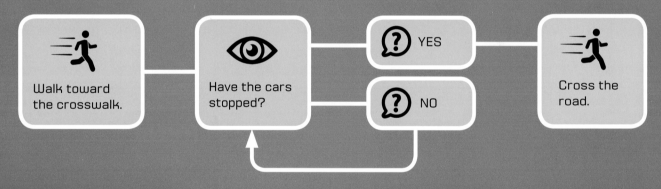

Computer programmers describe decision-making moments using IFTTT statements (if this, then that). For example, if there are no cars, then cross the road. Being programmed with multiple IFTTT statements would help the road-crossing robot know what to do in unusual situations, such as someone standing in its way in the crosswalk.

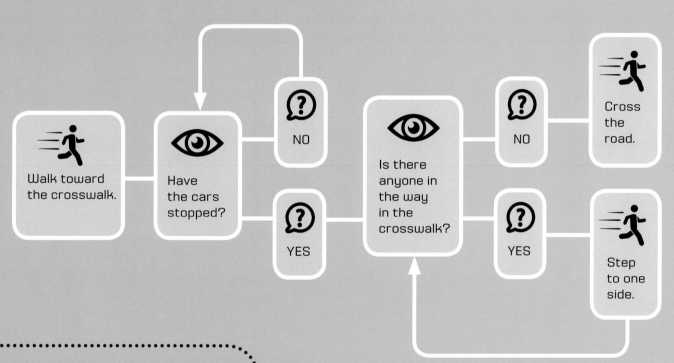

Walk toward the crosswalk.

Have the cars stopped?

NO

YES

Is there anyone in the way in the crosswalk?

NO

YES

Cross the road.

Step to one side.

THINKING OUTSIDE THE BOX!

Computer programmers can't anticipate every potential problem, so some robots need to be programmed to respond independently if things go wrong. Space rovers and robots in hostile environments far from humans are programmed to try random actions if they break or get stuck—eventually something should work!

ARTIFICIAL INTELLIGENCE

ARTIFICIAL INTELLIGENCE IS ONE OF THE MOST IMPORTANT AND CONTROVERSIAL AREAS OF ROBOTICS RESEARCH. MANY PEOPLE WONDER IF WE CAN OR SHOULD CREATE ROBOTS THAT CAN THINK FOR THEMSELVES.

It is hard to compare human and robot intelligence because they are both intelligent in different ways. Humans are intelligent because they can learn, reason, use language, and come up with new ideas. Robots can be programmed to be intelligent in some of these ways, such as learning. They learn by identifying and recording the results of specific actions. They know that if they repeat the action, it will have the same result. However, robots also have their own forms of intelligence, such as the ability to calculate complicated mathematical equations that most humans would never be able to solve.

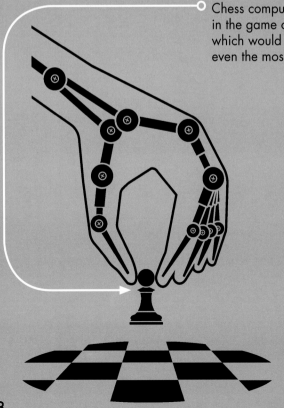

Chess computers are programmed to use reason to choose the best moves in the game of chess. They can consider the outcomes of all possible moves, which would be very hard for a human to do. Chess computers can beat even the most talented human chess players.

ENGINEERING TALK

The human brain is made up of an incredibly detailed network of electrical signals. Engineers believe that if they can create a complete map of the human brain and fully understand how it works, they might one day be able to create an artificial brain with a similar level of intelligence.

The Turing test is a way of testing the intelligence of robots. In the test, a human asks questions to another human and a robot via a computer screen, and tries to guess which is which. If the tester can't identify which is the human, then the robot passes the test. The problem with the Turing test is that it only tests whether robots can successfully imitate human ways of thinking. It doesn't test whether they can be programmed to truly think and feel for themselves.

TECHNOLOGY TALK

Most of the robots entered into the Turing test are chatbots. Chatbots are programmed to respond to standard questions by recognizing keywords and taking answers from a database. They are often used as automated customer service assistants to help people with simple problems online. Advanced chatbots learn more language from each conversation that they have with humans.

PROJECT

- Try chatting to a chatbot, such as the one found at http://alice.pandorabots.com/.

- Which type of question can the chatbot answer easily?

- Can you find a question that confuses the chatbot? Why is it confusing?

- What would be the difference between the chatbot's responses and a human's responses to the same questions?

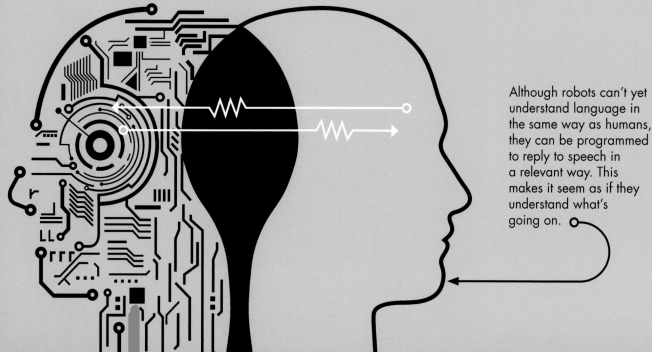

Although robots can't yet understand language in the same way as humans, they can be programmed to reply to speech in a relevant way. This makes it seem as if they understand what's going on.

ROBOT ETHICS

THERE ARE MANY DEBATES RELATED TO ROBOT **ETHICS**. MANY PEOPLE THINK THAT TRYING TO CONTROL NATURE MAY DO MORE HARM THAN GOOD. OTHERS WORRY ABOUT THE RESULTS OF CREATING ARTIFICIAL INTELLIGENCE.

Robots have already replaced thousands of human jobs in factories, such as in this car factory. If robots take over other types of jobs as well, it could have a devastating effect on employment around the world.

The main questions around robotics relate to the difference between humans and robots with advanced artificial intelligence. If we create robots that are as smart as humans, should the robots have the same rights as humans? Can we throw intelligent robots away if they are broken? Some people even fear that robots may one day become more intelligent than humans and take over human civilization. However, scientists haven't yet developed the technology that people are worrying about, so we have no real answers to these questions for now.

MATH TALK

Many industries are switching from human workers to robots in their factories. It costs more money to buy robots in the beginning. But it ends up being much cheaper than employing a human because people need to be paid a regular salary. If an industrial robot costs $50,000 to buy and a factory worker's salary is $1,200 a month, how many months will it take before the human worker's salary exceeds the cost of the robot?

Some people think that the key to resolving these ethical issues lies in the way that we program robots. Because humans are in charge of programming all robots, even super-intelligent ones, we can choose not to create robots that might put humans in danger. However, this is a difficult idea for some scientists to grasp because the thrill of making a breakthrough overshadows the outcomes of what they have created.

THINKING OUTSIDE THE BOX!

Scientist and author Isaac Asimov wrote many stories about robots. In one of his stories, Asimov introduced the Three Laws of Robotics. These are rules programmed into a robot's software that are designed to protect humans and ensure good robot behavior. Some people think that similar rules could help us control super-intelligent robots in the future.

Many science-fiction stories revolve around armies of robots rising up against humans, but this is very unlikely to happen in real life.

ASIMOV'S THREE LAWS OF ROBOTICS

FIRST LAW

A robot may not injure a human being or, through inaction, allow a human being to come to harm.

SECOND LAW

A robot must obey the orders given it by human beings except where such orders would conflict with the First Law.

THIRD LAW

A robot must protect its own existence as long as such protection does not conflict with the First or Second Laws.

THE FIRST ROBOTS

IN THE 18TH AND 19TH CENTURIES, THE ARRIVAL OF THE **INDUSTRIAL REVOLUTION** AND ELECTRICITY PAVED THE WAY FOR ROBOTICS. HOWEVER, IT WASN'T UNTIL THE 20TH CENTURY, AND THE RISE OF COMPUTERS AND COMPUTER PROGRAMMING, THAT THE FIRST ROBOTS BEGAN TO EMERGE.

For most of history, objects were made by hand, which was a time-consuming and expensive process. During the Industrial Revolution, people developed new machines that could manufacture objects for them, saving them time and money. Over time humans have learned to create more advanced machines, such as robots, that could do a lot of work with very little human input.

THINKING OUTSIDE THE BOX!

Weaving was one of the first industries to incorporate machines. Mechanical looms worked much faster than human weavers. In 1804 Joseph Marie Jacquard developed a machine that used punch cards to control the pattern of woven fabric. This invention inspired Charles Babbage, an early computer programmer. Babbage planned to use a similar system of punch cards to control his Analytical Engine, a type of early mechanical computer.

This is a modern model of one of Babbage's designs. The numbered wheels move around, allowing the machine to carry out complex mathematical equations.

As scientists learned how to handle electricity in the late 19th century, more and more machines were adapted to run off this new power source, including the first very simple robots. One of the first electrical robots, Elektro, appeared at the 1939 World's Fair in New York. Thanks to motors, Elektro could walk and move its arms and legs. An internal record player allowed Elektro to respond to a few simple voice commands.

Elektro later appeared with a robot dog, Sparko, that could sit, bark, and beg.

TECHNOLOGY TALK

The development of modern computers and computer programming in the 1940s and 1950s allowed robotics to flourish. Engineers learned how to use computers to control robots for different purposes. In 1954 the first industrial robot, Unimate, was introduced.
The robot was built by Unimation, the world's first robot manufacturing company. Unimate was a programmable robotic arm that could remove and stack hot metal parts in a factory.

The first computers were much larger than the computers we use today. This photo shows the ENIAC (Electronic Numerical Integrator and Computer), one of the first general-purpose computers. It went into use in 1946.

ROBOTS IN DANGER

Bomb-disposal robots have mechanical arms to pick up and inspect suspicious packages.

MANY JOBS CARRIED OUT BY ROBOTS ARE CONSIDERED TOO BORING FOR HUMANS. HOWEVER, ROBOTS ARE ALSO ON THE FRONTLINES IN SOME OF THE MOST DANGEROUS PLACES ON EARTH, WHERE HUMANS WOULD STRUGGLE TO SURVIVE.

Scientists often use robots to gather data in areas that humans can't reach, such as inside volcanoes or in deep underwater trenches. The data collected by these robots is crucial for scientists. One day this data might help scientists find evidence to explain things that we don't understand well, such as exactly how volcanoes erupt.

SCIENCE TALK

Using robots to gather data for experiments can help make it a fair test. When people carry out experiments, it's possible that they might accidentally do something differently each time, which would affect the results. Because robots can't change their behavior unless they are programmed to do so, the conditions of a robot-led experiment will always be the same. This keeps results accurate.

This looks like a toy, but it's actually a NASA SnoMote robot. This robot takes measurements in remote polar regions. Scientists study this data to try to understand why the ice is melting so fast in these areas.

Robots can also be used to resolve very dangerous situations where human lives would be at risk. Robots are routinely used to dispose of bombs and find land mines. They have also been used to explore areas affected by earthquakes and other disasters. Tiny robots can squeeze into small gaps in the rubble of collapsed buildings to look for survivors.

This bomb-disposal robot is investigating an abandoned bag in case it contains explosive material.

THINKING OUTSIDE THE BOX!

When designing a robot, it can help to think about who or what typically uses the environment where the robot will be operated. For example, a robot designed to clear up nuclear waste in a nuclear power plant will need to move through an environment designed for humans: walking up stairs, opening doors with handles and using tools designed for humans. As a result, this robot probably needs to be humanoid, with jointed legs to walk up stairs and jointed fingers to hold door handles and tools.

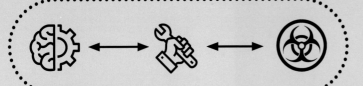

PROJECT

- Design a robot that can explore the peaks of extremely high mountains.

- Which animals live high on mountains? How can you use their movement and body shape as inspiration?

- What kind of sensors would work best in mountainous conditions?

ROBOTS IN SPACE

HUMANS USE ROBOTS TO EXPLORE AREAS OF OUTER SPACE THAT THEY ARE NOT YET ABLE TO VISIT. ROBOTIC ROVERS HAVE VISITED MARS, VENUS, AND SEVERAL ASTEROIDS AND COMETS.

Space rovers are robotic vehicles that explore, take measurements, and snap photos. They can analyze the chemical composition of rock samples so that scientists on Earth know what the surface is made of. Many rovers are powered by **radioactive** materials because it can be risky to depend on solar power. The *Philae* lander went into sleep mode after landing in a shady area on a comet because it couldn't get enough sunlight to power itself.

MATH TALK

Scientists communicate with rovers in space via radio waves. However, most bodies in space are very far away from Earth, so it takes a long time for radio waves to arrive. As a result, scientists can't control rovers in real time. Most rover activity is automated or programmed in advance. We can use a distance/speed/time triangle to figure out how long communication will take.

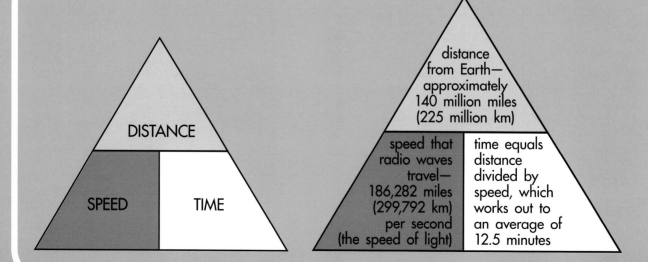

DISTANCE

SPEED | TIME

distance from Earth—approximately 140 million miles (225 million km)

speed that radio waves travel—186,282 miles (299,792 km) per second (the speed of light)

time equals distance divided by speed, which works out to an average of 12.5 minutes

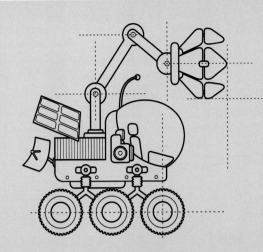

Scientists do not always have a complete understanding of the environment that a rover will be exploring. So they need to prepare the robot to move over different types of **terrain**. Most rovers have large wheels that are from 2 feet (65 cm) long to 10 feet (3 meters) long. Theses sturdy wheels work well on rugged, rocky ground. Engineers are also experimenting with other types of movement, such as a jumping robot that could leap out of deep sand.

Robonaut is a **humanoid** robot that works on the International Space Station. It has fully functioning fingers that allow it to do many of the same tasks as the astronauts.

THINKING OUTSIDE THE BOX!

It would be risky not to test rovers, but it is expensive and time-consuming to test them in space. Instead, engineers test robots and train astronauts in places called analog sites, where the conditions are very similar to space. Analog sites can be icy or boiling hot to match different temperatures in space. They also have sandy, rocky, or steep surfaces to mimic a planet's surface.

ENGINEERING TALK

Rovers are designed to fix themselves because there are no humans around to repair them if they break down in space. For example, if a drill bit on the *Curiosity* Mars rover gets stuck in a rock, the drill arm spits it out. The drill arm then picks up a replacement drill bit from a storage box, pops it into place, and keeps on drilling!

DRONES AND CARS

THE IDEA OF LETTING ROBOTIC VEHICLES NAVIGATE OUR ROADS AND AIRWAYS IS BECOMING MORE AND MORE ACCEPTABLE. DRONES AND SELF-DRIVING CARS CAN GREATLY BENEFIT HUMANS, BUT THERE IS ALWAYS A RISK INVOLVED.

A drone is an aircraft without a pilot on board. Most drones are controlled remotely by programming in a GPS location and letting the drone figure out how to get there. At first drones were mainly used by the military to observe the enemy, transport weapons, and drop bombs. But since drones have become cheaper and more available, they've been used in other ways. For example, drones have been used to deliver items, carry out research, or just for fun.

Can you identify the landscapes shown in these aerial photos taken by drones?

ART TALK

Videos mounted on drones have captured amazing **aerial** images that show us the world from an often unseen angle. As we focus on the shapes and patterns, many landscapes look quite different when seen from above. These images could be an interesting starting point for a work of art.

In theory, self-driving cars are advanced enough to be able to navigate the streets on their own. But for safety reasons, there are no driverless cars on the streets yet. For now, engineers are testing self-driving cars with humans behind the wheel who can take over just in case. However, self-driving cars have been involved in several crashes, including one in which the human passenger died. So scientists still have a ways to go.

Google is investing a lot of money in self-driving cars, and is hoping to make them available to the public by 2020.

ENGINEERING TALK

Self-driving cars have various sensors that allow them to find their way around the roads. They use cameras to recognize signs, radar to figure out the amount of space between them and nearby vehicles, and lasers to gather data on the car's surroundings. These sensors send data to the onboard computer, which is programmed to decide how to drive the car. This computer will instruct the car to slow down or speed up, if necessary.

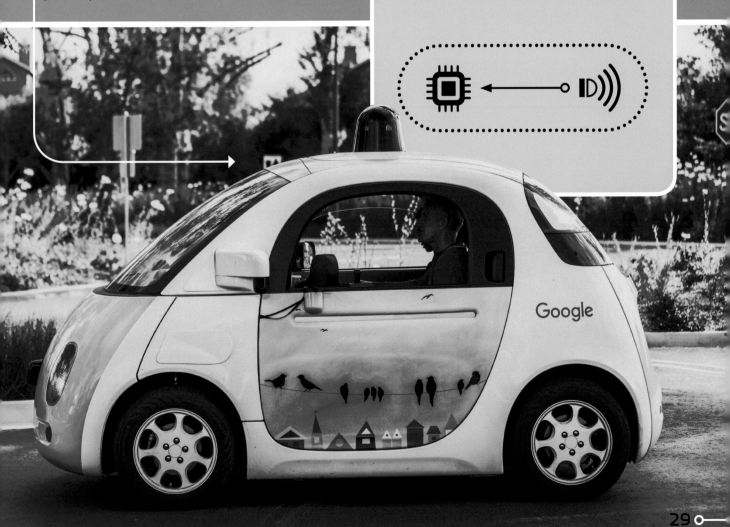

ROBOTICS ENGINEERS AROUND THE WORLD ARE CONSTANTLY CREATING IMPRESSIVE ROBOTS TO CARRY OUT CERTAIN JOBS OR TO TEST NEW TECHNOLOGY.

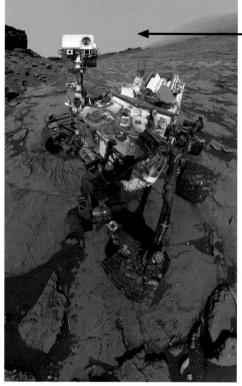

CURIOSITY ROVER

The world's most-famous robotic rover, NASA's *Curiosity*, is currently exploring Mars. It is looking for evidence of water and checking to see if Mars might have the right conditions for humans to survive there in the future. NASA streams footage from *Curiosity*'s adventures, which many people have enjoyed watching on the Internet.
On the first anniversary of *Curiosity*'s stay on Mars, it played the song "Happy Birthday." It was the first time a song was played on another planet.

ASIMO

ASIMO is one of the most advanced humanoid robots. It is used in public demonstrations around the world as an example of what can be achieved in robotics. ASIMO has two legs and can walk and run, which is a huge achievement in robotics. It can also recognize gestures, sounds, and faces and can use this information to interact with humans.

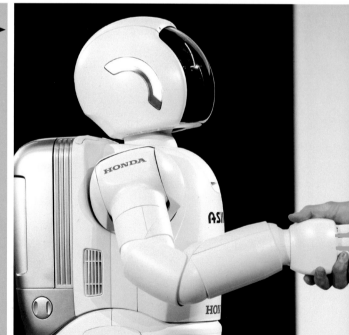

○ ROBOTIC STINGRAY

This real stingray was the inspiration for a **cyborg** stingray. The robotic stingray has more than 200,000 **genetically engineered** rat heart-muscle **cells** on its underside. When the heart cells contract like they do in humans to pump blood around the body, the movement pushes the cyborg stingray forward in the water! The heart cells are also genetically engineered so that they only contract in certain light. Scientists can control where the robot moves by shining light in different places. They hope to learn more about how the heart pumps blood from experiments with the cyborg stingray.

○ ROBOBEE

These mini-robots weigh less than 0.004 ounces (0.1 grams) and are half the length of a paper clip. Yet they could aid in search-and-rescue missions and even help grow crops. Robobees are able to act as a group and coordinate their behavior, just like a swarm of real bees. Their tiny wings are made of a ceramic material that expands and contracts when electricity passes through it. This creates a flapping motion that keeps the robobees in the air.

LS3 ○

This powerful robot is designed to carry equipment for soldiers (LS3 stands for Legged Squad Support System). Similar to a horse, the LS3 can follow a leader through all terrain while avoiding obstacles and carrying around 400 pounds (180 kg) of cargo. Having a helper to carry equipment keeps soldiers from getting tired or hurting themselves before the fighting has even begun.

WHILE THE LATEST DEVELOPMENTS IN ROBOTICS DAZZLE US ON TV, EQUALLY IMPRESSIVE ROBOTS CAN ALSO BE FOUND IN OUR HOMES. ROBOTIC TOYS, HOUSEHOLD APPLIANCES, AND COMPANIONS BRING CONVENIENCE AND ENJOYMENT TO OUR DAY-TO-DAY LIVES.

ROOMBA

The Roomba is an **autonomous** robot vacuum cleaner. It's actually quite unusual to have a fully autonomous robot. Most robots are semi-autonomous for safety reasons. However, the Roomba is so small that it isn't considered a risk to let it do its own thing. It uses sensors to detect especially dirty areas and know when to change direction. It can even sense deep drops to prevent it from falling down stairs.

PARO THE SEAL

In some hospitals and nursing homes, Paro robot seals are given to patients to soothe them and keep them company. Paro can seek out eye contact and respond to stroking and sounds, including its own name. It's also covered in soft white fur that people love to touch!

FURBY

These adorable, fluffy toys are actually tiny robots! Although Furbies start out speaking only in Furbish, a unique Furby language, their internal computer is programmed to "learn" English words through interaction with humans. A simple motor system allows the Furby to raise its eyelids and ears and open its mouth.

LEGO™ MINDSTORMS

Many people feel that the best way to learn about robots is by building them with kits like Lego™ Mindstorms. This range of Lego™ kits contains the software and hardware needed to build your own robot. It includes a mini computer, sensors, motors, and circuits.

AIBO

This robotic dog is designed to behave just like a real pet. Aibo can run and jump, react to its surroundings, and show emotions, such as joy. This makes it an excellent stand-in for a real dog, despite its $1,700 price tag. Aibo was first released in 1999 (shown here). But in 2006 the company that made Aibo stopped production. In 2018 Sony brought Aibo back with updated features, such as the ability to take photos, an app, and a new line of tricks.

JIBO

The social robot Jibo is creating a lot of buzz! Jibo was designed by Cynthia Breazeal, a pioneer in the field of robot-human social interaction. Jibo is programmed to have meaningful social interactions with people and become a real part of the family. In addition to keeping track of appointments, Jibo can tell stories, take photos, and recognize faces and voices.

ROBOTS AND MEDICINE

USING ROBOTS IN MEDICINE CAN HELP MAKE SURGERIES AND MEDICAL PROCEDURES SAFER, CHEAPER, AND MORE EFFICIENT. HOWEVER, DOCTORS HAVE TO BE VERY CAUTIOUS BECAUSE IF A ROBOT BREAKS DOWN, IT COULD PUT THE PATIENT'S LIFE IN DANGER.

The da Vinci surgical robot is one of the most successful medical robots, with more than 3,000 models used in hospitals around the world. It is used for keyhole surgeries in which tools are pushed through a very small hole in the skin to reach areas deep inside the body. The da Vinci robot is incredibly precise and will never shake or get distracted, unlike a human surgeon.

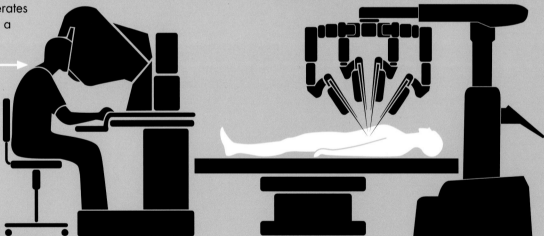

A surgeon operates on a patient using a da Vinci robot.

PROJECT

- The da Vinci robot is so accurate that it can stitch a grape back together after it has been cut open. Ask an adult to help you cut a grape open and then try stitching it back together with a needle and thread.

- How easy is it?

- What features could a robot have that would make it better at this type of activity than a human?

THINKING OUTSIDE THE BOX!

Safety is a big concern with medical robots. Most robots can't make autonomous decisions and can only respond in the way that they have been programmed. So who would be held responsible if something went wrong? To resolve this ethical issue, surgeons control surgical robots at all times. Robots that transport medicine around hospitals are programmed with codes and fingerprint sensors so that the medicine will only be released to the correct person.

TECHNOLOGY TALK

Surgeons control surgical robots using a computer or a telemanipulator. A telemanipulator is a device that transmits movements made by the surgeon to the robot electronically or mechanically. Surgeons can also control robots directly through a computer. This is particularly useful because it means that the surgeon can be thousands of miles away from the robot.

Robots are useful when training doctors. Instead of using real patients, doctors can practice on patient simulator robots, which can breathe, bleed, and sweat just like humans. They can also mimic the symptoms of a heart attack or a seizure. Practicing on robots reduces the risk to real patients because a real patient won't be harmed if the doctor makes a mistake.

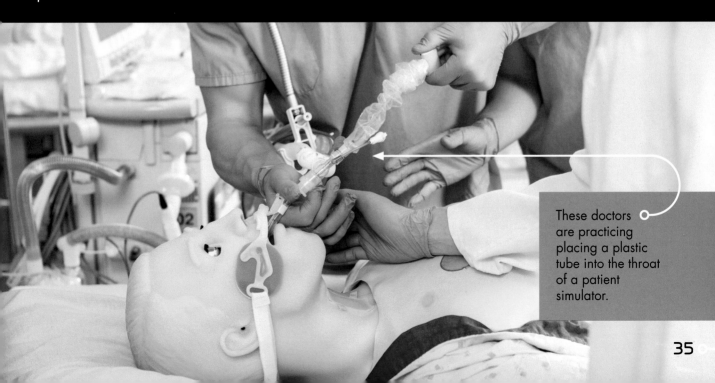

These doctors are practicing placing a plastic tube into the throat of a patient simulator.

BIONICS

BIONICS ARE ROBOTIC REPLACEMENTS FOR BIOLOGICAL BODY PARTS. ADVANCES IN BIONICS ARE ON TRACK TO REVOLUTIONIZE MEDICINE. FOR EXAMPLE, IF WE COULD CREATE ROBOTIC ORGANS, WE WOULDN'T NEED TO DEPEND ON HUMAN DONORS.

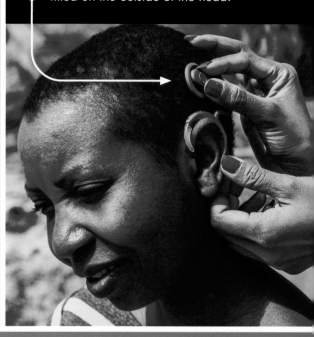

The microphone of the cochlear implant is fitted on the outside of the head.

The cochlear implant is one of the most commonly used bionics. Instead of standard hearing aids, which just make sounds louder, cochlear implants allow people with hearing problems to hear. A microphone in the implant picks up sounds and converts them into electrical impulses. The implant then sends the impulses to the brain, where they are interpreted as sounds.

SCIENCE TALK

Sounds are waves of vibrations that travel through the air and into our ears. The cochlear implant carries out the same function as the snail-shaped cochlea inside the ear. They both convert vibrations into signals, which are then sent to the brain and understood as sound.

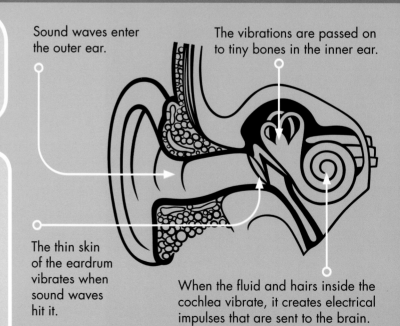

Sound waves enter the outer ear.

The vibrations are passed on to tiny bones in the inner ear.

The thin skin of the eardrum vibrates when sound waves hit it.

When the fluid and hairs inside the cochlea vibrate, it creates electrical impulses that are sent to the brain.

Bionic eyes work using an implant in the retina, the inner layer of the surface of the eye. They can help people who have lost their vision due to illness. The implant receives visual information from a miniature camera that is worn as part of a pair of glasses. This information is then passed on to the brain. The bionic eye is still being developed and can't see detailed images just yet, but it can recognize outlines, which is a huge step forward.

BEFORE

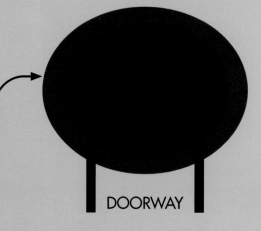

DOORWAY

AFTER

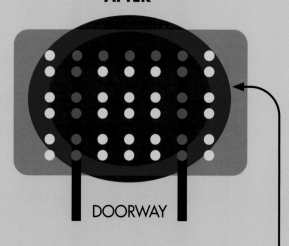

DOORWAY

Someone with vision loss due to illness wouldn't be able to see the line of a doorway. Everything would appear black.

After being fitted with a bionic eye, someone with vision loss would be able to make out the shape of a doorway against a wall.

SCIENCE TALK

The bionic artificial heart is currently being used as a temporary solution while people wait for a heart transplant. The engineering behind it is very simple, as the heart is essentially a pump! When it squeezes in, blood is pushed out around the body.

PROJECT

- Design a bionic lung.
- What are the functions of the lung?
- How would the bionic lung work mechanically?
- What materials would you use to make the bionic lung?

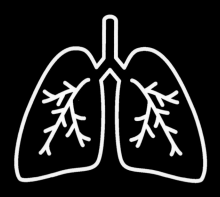

ROBOTIC ARMS

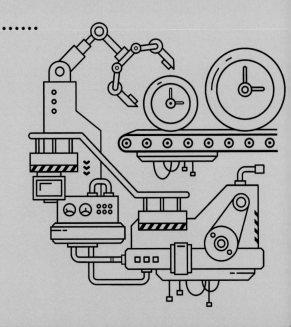

ROBOTS IN FACTORIES AND ASSEMBLY LINES OFTEN NEED TO PICK UP OBJECTS. ENGINEERS BUILD ROBOTS WITH SIMPLIFIED VERSIONS OF HUMAN HANDS, WHICH ARE CONTROLLED BY COMPUTERS TO MAKE THE ROBOT GRASP AND GRIP.

The human hand is pretty unbeatable as a tool, so it's easy to understand why engineers have copied its design. The 27 bones in the hand give us a wide range of movements. The sensors on the tip of our fingers send signals to the brain that give us important information about the objects that we touch.

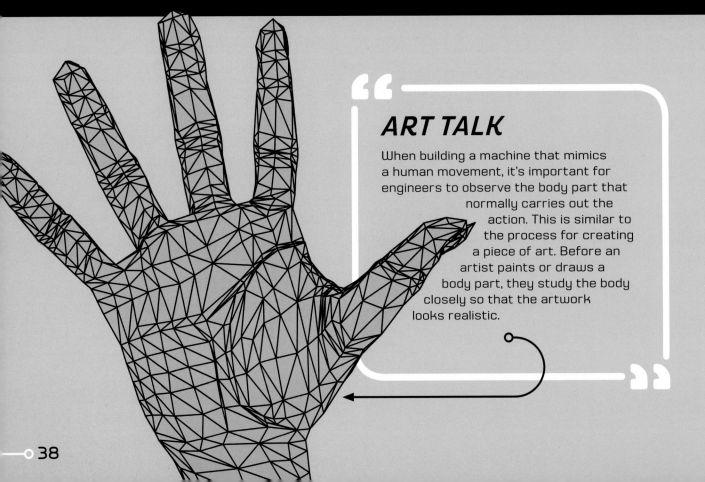

" ART TALK

When building a machine that mimics a human movement, it's important for engineers to observe the body part that normally carries out the action. This is similar to the process for creating a piece of art. Before an artist paints or draws a body part, they study the body closely so that the artwork looks realistic. "

THINKING OUTSIDE THE BOX!

It would be unnecessary and expensive to give a complex robotic hand to a robot that has a simple task to do, such as picking up bottles. Instead, engineers give robots basic versions of human hands with two or three "fingers" to pinch and hold, or special attachments, such as hooks, suction cups, or magnets!

One step beyond the robotic hand is the robotic **prosthetic** arm, which can replace a limb lost through disease or injury. Instead of being controlled by a computer, robotic prosthetic arms are directly controlled by the human brain. Thoughts from the brain are captured and turned into movement (see Technology Talk). The arm can also feel and touch, which helps the user interact with his or her surroundings.

TECHNOLOGY TALK

Wires connect robotic prosthetic arms with the motor cortex of the brain, which controls muscle movement. Thoughts from the brain, which are tiny electrical charges, travel down the wires and make the arm move. When the fingers touch something, the arm sends electrical signals to the sensory cortex in the brain. The signals are then interpreted the as the feeling of touch.

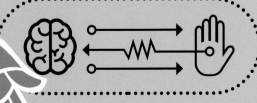

ANDROIDS

ANDROIDS ARE ROBOTS THAT ARE DESIGNED TO LOOK AND ACT EXACTLY LIKE HUMANS. FOR MANY YEARS, REALISTIC ANDROIDS ONLY EXISTED IN SCIENCE FICTION. BUT MODERN SCIENTISTS ARE GETTING CLOSER TO DESIGNING LIFELIKE ROBOTIC HUMANS.

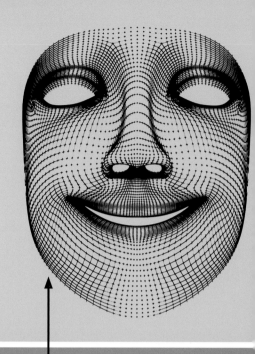

Robot designers use engineering and programming to make androids appear to have emotions, just like humans. Tiny artificial muscles controlled by motors are placed on the android's face. The muscles are programmed to move to create different facial expressions when the robot senses that it is the appropriate moment, using visual or spoken clues.

An android may make a happy face when it picks up words such as *happy* or *good*. It might also do so when its facial recognition software notices that another person has a happy expression on his or her face.

SCIENCE TALK

Unlike cyborgs, which contain real biological parts such as muscles or nerves, androids are totally **synthetic**. To make androids look realistic, scientists cover them in synthetic materials, such as soft, flexible silicone jelly, that look very similar to real human skin.

The Geminoid android (left) is modeled after a real person (right). The robot designers copied everything from him, including his movements and gestures.

People often find it easier to relate to robots if they have human faces. They are happier to interact with them and find them less intimidating than typical machines. However, robot designers need to be careful because androids can look very creepy if they look too much like humans.

PROJECT

- With the help of an adult, find 10 pictures of 3D computer-generated human faces on the Internet, and put them in order from least humanlike to most humanlike.

- Do any of the faces seem creepy to you?

- Where do they appear on the scale?

- Show the images to some friends, and compare their reactions to your own.

0 1 2 3 4 5 6 7 8 9 10

" ART TALK

Human faces are one of the hardest things to get right when drawing, painting, or sculpting, and it's no easier for a robot designer. Using proportion will make your artwork look more realistic. For example, the width of a head is about the same as five eyes in a row.

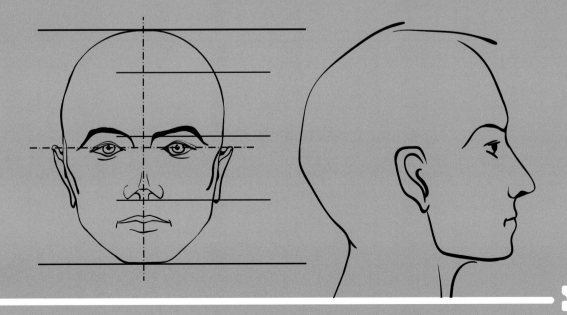

HALL OF FAME: FICTIONAL ROBOTS

MANY OF OUR IDEAS ABOUT WHAT ROBOTS ARE LIKE COME FROM FICTIONAL ROBOTS FROM BOOKS, FILMS, AND TV SHOWS. THE WORD *ROBOT* EVEN COMES FROM A PLAY THAT WAS WRITTEN BY CZECH PLAYWRIGHT ǨAREL CAPEK IN 1920.

ROBBY THE ROBOT

This robot from the 1956 film *Forbidden Planet* was one of the first robots in film that had its own personality. Robby worked as a servant but also enjoyed cooking food such as space donuts. For many years, Robby's shape inspired people's views of what a robot should look like.

C-3PO, R2-D2 AND BB-8

These three droids—the name for robots in the *Star Wars* universe—are designed to help their owners with various tasks. R2-D2 and BB-8 can repair and maintain spaceships. C-3PO is an expert at translating languages and explaining foreign customs.

WALL-E

In the film of the same name, WALL-E is a trash compactor robot that is left to clear up a polluted Earth at some point in the future. Although WALL-E is programmed to carry out his duties, he also has a personality and hobbies, such as collecting things and owning a pet. These human characteristics make robots such as WALL-E appeal more to us.

TERMINATOR

This cyborg assassin from the *Terminator* films has no human emotions, but it is nearly impossible to tell him apart from a human. He even sweats and bleeds. The *Terminator* films are set in a future where there is a war going on between robots and humans. The Terminator fights on the side of the robots.

DALEK AND K-9

These robots from the *Doctor Who* TV series appear at opposite ends of the good/evil spectrum! Daleks are evil, robotic cyborgs, made up of biological alien parts and artificial robot parts. The only emotion they can feel is hate, which makes them a serious threat. Meanwhile, K-9 is a friendly robotic dog that makes an excellent companion to Doctor Who, just like a real pet dog.

OPTIMUS PRIME

This giant robot from the *Transformers* films and toys offers two looks for the price of one. It can transform from a robot into a giant semitruck. Optimus Prime is dedicated to fighting evil robots so that robots and humans can live together peacefully.

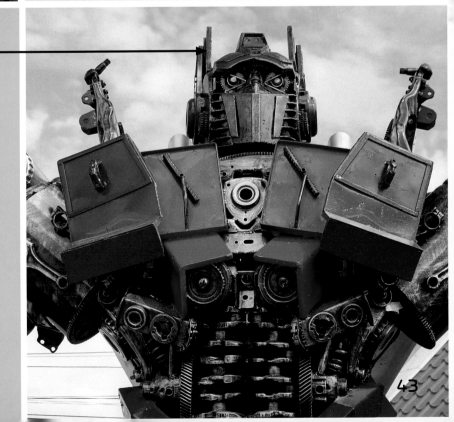

ROBOTS OF THE FUTURE

ROBOTICS HAS COME A LONG WAY IN THE PAST 50 YEARS. ENGINEERS HAVE MADE ROBOTS BETTER AT THE JOBS WE NEED THEM TO DO AND DEVELOPED THEM FOR JOBS WE WOULD LIKE THEM TO DO. IT SEEMS LIKELY THAT THE NEXT 50 YEARS WILL BRING SIMILAR PROGRESS.

The study of very, very tiny robots, or nanobots, is an area of robot research that could have an incredible impact on healthcare. Scientists believe that tiny robots could be programmed to go directly to areas with cancer cells and destroy them or repair damaged tissue inside the body. Because the nanobots could be programmed only to target certain areas, they would help patients recover faster and more effectively.

Scientists are looking into the possibility of a robotic red blood cell that could transport more oxygen around the body than biological red blood cells. This could help people with blood diseases or boost athletic performance.

MATH TALK

Nanobots measure between 4 microinches and 400 microinches (0.1 and 10 micrometers). In comparison, the width of a strand of spiderweb silk is around 118 microinches (3 micrometers). A microinch is a division of an inch. There are a million microinches in 1 inch. How many microinches are there in a foot?

One of the greatest future challenges for scientists and robotics engineers is to perfect how to program robots to behave in a typically human way. They have already created a robot nanny named Pepper. Pepper was designed to babysit children and can adjust its behavior depending on the child's emotions. In the future robots may be able to master jobs that require high levels of social interaction, such as teaching or working on the police force.

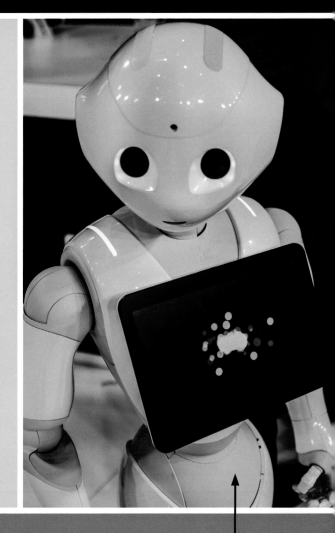

ENGINEERING TALK

To recognize human emotions, Pepper uses sound sensors and facial recognition software to identify **tone** of voice and facial expressions. The robot refers to a database of common results to recognize the emotion shown and is programmed to react accordingly.

Pepper can respond to a human's emotions by displaying special symbols on its tablet and changing the tone of its voice.

THINKING OUTSIDE THE BOX!

Many jobs that once belonged to humans may be lost to robots in the future. But the growth of the robotics industry will also create new jobs. People with the right skills will be needed to design, test, and build the robots of the future.

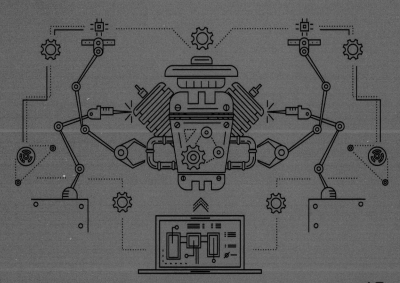

 GLOSSARY

aerial (AYR-ee-uhl)—having to do with things that are high in the air

android (AN-droid)—a robot that looks like a human, with lifelike skin and a face that moves

artificial intelligence (ar-ti-FISH-uhl in-TEL-uh-junss)—the ability of a machine to think like a person

autonomous (aw-TAH-nuh-muhs)—able to respond, react, or develop independently

biological (bye-uh-LAH-ji-kuhl)—having to do with living things

cell (SEL)—the smallest unit of living things

code (KODE)—the instructions of a computer program

cyborg (CYE-borg)—a robot that is a combination of biological and mechanical parts

database (DAY-tuh-bays)—a group of computer files that organizes and stores information

electrical circuit (i-LEK-tri-kuhl SUR-kuht)—the path that electricity flows through

ethics (ETH-iks)—having to do with right and wrong

genetically engineered (juh-NET-ik-lee en-juh-NEERD)—having genes that have been changed to produce certain characteristics

GPS (Global Positioning System) (GLOH-buhl puh-ZI-shuh-ning SISS-tuhm)—an electronic tool used to find the location of an object

humanoid (HYOO-muh-noid)—a robot that looks or acts like a human

Industrial Revolution (in-DUHSS-tree-uhl rev-uh-LOO-shuhn)—a period from 1790 to 1860 when work began to be done by machines, rather than by hand

interact (in-tur-AKT)—to talk or do things with other people

molecule (MOL-uh-kyool)—two or more atoms bonded together

navigate (NAV-uh-gate)—to decide on a direction for travel

parallel (PA-ruh-lel)—an equal distance apart at all points

program (PROH-gram)—to enter a series of step-by-step instructions into a computer or robot to tell it what to do

proprioception (pro-pree-oh-SEP-shuhn)—the sense of where your own body is positioned and how it moves

prosthetic (pross-THET-ik)—an artificial device that replaces a missing body part

prototype (PROH-tuh-tipe)—the first version of an invention that tests an idea to see if it will work

radioactive (ray-dee-oh-AK-tiv)—giving off potentially harmful invisible rays or particles

sensor (SEN-sur)—a device that detects changes, such as heat, light, sound, or motion

sonar (SOH-nar)—a device that uses sound waves to sense or detect objects

synthetic (sin-THET-ik)—something that is manufactured or artificial rather than found in nature

terrain (tuh-RAYN)—the surface of the land

tone (TOHN)—a way of speaking or writing that shows a certain feeling or attitude

READ MORE

Baum, Margaux. *Engineering and Building Robots for Competitions.* Hands-On Robotics. New York: Rosen Publishing, 2018.

Lepora, Nathan. *Robots*. DK Find Out! New York: DK Publishing, 2018.

Lindeen, Mary. *Drones and Flying Robots.* Cutting-Edge Robotics. Minneapolis, Minn.: Lerner Publications, 2018.

INTERNET SITES

Use FactHound to find Internet sites related to this book.

Visit www.facthound.com

Just type in 9781543532319 and go.

 Check out projects, games and lots more at
www.capstonekids.com

QUIZ

- **Why do robots in space often run on solar power?**

- **Who wrote the Three Laws of Robotics?**

- **Name two ways in which the military uses drones.**

- **What animal does Paro look like?**

- **Which fictional robot has a job picking up trash?**

INDEX

QUIZ ANSWERS

- They can't connect to electrical outlets or have their batteries replaced.

- Isaac Asimov

- Some uses include observing the enemy, carrying weapons, and dropping bombs.

- A seal

- WALL-E